DARK ROOTS

poems by

Caroline Malone

Finishing Line Press
Georgetown, Kentucky

DARK ROOTS

For Julia, who always inspires and who never gives up on me.

ACKNOWLEDGMENTS

Some of these poems appeared in the following publications:

Boulevard
Heartwood
The Dos Passos Review
Spaces

Publisher: Leah Maines
Editor: Christen Kincaid
Cover Art: Caroline Malone
Author Photo: Caroline Malone
Cover Design: Elizabeth Maines McCleavy

Printed in the USA on acid-free paper.
Order online: www.finishinglinepress.com
             also available on amazon.com

Author inquiries and mail orders:
Finishing Line Press
P. O. Box 1626
Georgetown, Kentucky 40324
U. S. A.

Table of Contents

Undertaking

Civil War

Thin Places

UNDERTAKING

Secret City

In the secret city I was a prisoner of safety.
My new world was opened at the Elza Gate
with a cherry bomb that produced a cloud,
the explosion a symbol of what was to come.
The streetlamps burned like new stars,
guard towers rose to equal the height of the oaks,
and barbed-wire rolled like bales of hay
topped the fence surrounding Oak Ridge.
Nights, I listened for the buzz of enemy planes
while the breeze shook the lilac bush against my window.
I was safe because my father slept in the room
next to mine, his identity badge hung from the bed post,
the combination to his office safe locked in his head.
Out in the living room, black and white stills of mushroom clouds
decorated the walls, their captions placing them in time:
"Los Alamos, Hansford, The Trinity Test, The 'Little Boy' bomb."
My father had his hands in the elements, on the pen
of authority to alter someone's face for peace.
At night, he came home and was silent at his desk,
both as close and as distant as the enemy cities in Japan,
his face and hands red as the sun with anger
over what was a mystery to me.
But that isn't true.
He wasn't my father; he was my grandfather
who raised me after my mother and father moved on.
And I didn't live in the 1940s. I was born in 1961.
Yet my grandfather was history, and he brought the bombs
and codes with him into my life, and he raised me in his secret city.
Now he's dead and some nights I look into the sky
to scan for enemy planes. I listen for the whir
of propellers and wonder where my grandfather is.

Persephone to Demeter

Mother, I have grown to see
the darkness as a blood-black jewel;
such are the bruises that adorn my body.
Under the cream of my skin
each one spreads its fury into a crown.

And this, my custom to the pitch
of the underworld—not a getting used to,
not even a compromise,
but rather, the absence of light
illuminates the truth of my nature;
see how I blend to escape you,
see me pursue my shadow
who runs in fright of my roses,
my shadow pure as the obsidian
that cools my neck. Just look
at the treasures in the ground
my love has saved for me:
necklace of bone, bracelet of hair.

This is why you withhold in grief
abundance from the earth;
you see your daughter for what she really is—
the mine's vein that pulses with gold,
royalty to consume your bounty.
Feast in the night of her throat.

Even Song

Already spirit, I lived beside my mother's body
as it fought the tubes, the pump, the thin wire
the physician had inserted believing it could know
her heart well enough to keep her alive.
How familiar her silence, how perfectly normal
her caregivers' assumptions.
Day one: She is the sickest person here.
Day two: Her chart status reads grim.
Day three: She has had a bad day.
Predictable love appeared as the nurses insisted
on tidying her up, so I could say goodbye
to the person they thought I knew.
A second kind of love arrested me:
There was death and that small blue cross
in your hand, the stranger, so beautifully still,
so quiet, so confident in her prayers,
my only fear in the room.

Resignation

Years ago, when we laid you to rest, I marked your grave with memory:
the thought of roses and daffodils, of the Southern rattling on the tracks.

I know the stone, your name and dates carved in the marble
the two maple trees guarding at your sides.

I returned when I was older and kneeled with the dirt in my mind,
competing with the words, competing with the poem,
competing with the grass, waiting,

for it to mature, to bend over me as the arms of the mother
embrace the child, and grow quietly into the ground on the other side.

Fragments

In the shadow of the Acropolis of Athens we walk above the ruins,
all that was once hidden within the earth, now clearly beneath us,
houses, roads, baths, and workshops, remains of sacrificial ritual pyres
seen through a glass floor, protected from the feet of travelers.
Inside, case after case of vessels, the flat alabastron,
the false-mouthed amphora, urns of the cremated,
schematized birds fluttering across the bronze.
Ankle bones of small animals children used to play games,
crotalistria for the gods, and the red-figure krater funeral procession.
Walls of sections of marble body parts: a breast, eyes, an ear, a leg
inserted into carved niches of limestone pillars, offerings to Asclepius
for curing the diseased members. The young women in relief,
dancing, their heavily folded himations lightly raised off the ground,
missing feet, missing arms, still moving imperceptibly to a sound.

The Idea of Things

We are looking out the windows at the first snow,
wondering why so many people find it amazing
when the cats say it's simply a form of water,
that the flakes falling is temporarily interesting
but not nearly as exciting as the cardinals and jays
swooping from the sky to the bird feeder,
their wings beating with precision for the perfect landing.
The Siberian Husky begs to come in after
the ground is sufficiently white, the grass
no longer green on any side, so I open the door
and the dog scampers in, which is the movement
of a little pup and not an arctic athlete.
The streets are still black and the garbage truck
still makes its rounds while school children in the holler
pull the covers back over their heads or drag out
saucers and mittens to barrel down the rolling hills.
Global warming is to blame for the lack of muscular winters
like those of our youth when my father slipped
on the frozen driveway and busted his ribs,
or when we flew down the steepest road for miles,
iron runners scraping and screeching on the ice,
narrowly avoiding a head-on with a telephone poll
at the bottom of the run.
                            These were things we did
without thinking, without premeditation or fear,
these were things we saw and tasted and felt
without prediction or expectation or idea
they would be memories.

Trace

Just before reaching the grassy bald
Soul threatened to abandon me,
Stealing the sunny path out of the woods,
The last mottled markers on the switch back trail.
Soul stretched out its stride ahead of me,
Breaking into pieces the brittle fall
Leaves beneath its steps
Inhaling the musky scent of the galaxy
Emitting its cloud of decomposing sulfur,
The balsamic buds steeped like tea,
Tasting the sour red clusters of mountain ash berries,
Knowing that buried in the dense undergrowth
There would be not even bones to mark our parting.

After Hours

Just the taxis now on 47th
limping home after the celebration that was Saturday night.
From the fifth floor their metal bodies
sound like waves washing against a shore.
In the city now, no conga line, no tiny umbrellas
floating in glasses, no poets competing with images,
no poets in arms over the death of their art,
no poets cursing publishing, the free market,
the lie that is democracy. No. They said goodbye
to a friend the only way they knew how:
they drained the bar of Stoli,
they emptied their hearts of joy,
they renounced their duties as keepers of visions
and followed home the trash lining the streets
for the promise of warm beds and sleep.

And there you are just five blocks removed,
thirty floors away from all that remains
of the sirens, the drunken laughter, the echoing bottle
in the gutter, the man yelling, *Muthafuckah*,
into the dark, and from the poet
who was early this morning
tenderly and thankfully delivered to her door
by friends who only hours before found silence
the only answer to the loss of words.

This should be the time we know
the comforts of the distances we have travelled,
and it does not matter, my love, which city we are in,
you who are always at least a mile away,
not far enough to make the walk impossible,
too close to pretend you are out of reach.

Turn Out

Months he has been mine,
weeks of slogging through the rutted mud,
muck boots caked, slipping and sticking
in the drenched earth after hours of rain
saturated ground glutted with manure,
days of sweat in the damp thick air,
first chasing and cornering, next sweet talking
then sinking to the sparse brittle timothy
waiting out his stubborn or mischievous moods,
halter over my shoulder and the lead
stained with blood from my sliced flesh
where his brute bucking ripped the rope across my palm.
Leading him on the gravel lane lined
with the same damn scrubby pines that harbor
beasts, antediluvian creatures ready to pounce;
he rolls his eyes, stiffens his ears, jigs into my side
coming close to knocking me flat. But I coo,
stroke his withers, throw back my shoulders
and walk with purpose as he picks up his pace.
Brush and clusters of late blooming heal-all
yield to a breeze, flutter and settle
when a starling darts from the hedge
into our path. We start and stop, trying to follow
its flight as it glides and dips to the hilltop beyond.

Resistance

Driving on the back roads of a cool spring afternoon,
a canopy of green leaves and their shadows filtering a brilliant sun,
I see it on the center line, a possum frozen in that fatal moment
when the car tires struck the body and continued its journey
down the same road with a canopy of green leaves and their shadows.
As I neared the body, a gang of shiny crows, sleek and glowing, waiting
on the oil slick blacktop challenged me to displace them
from the carcass they had claimed and almost stripped bare,
the tough beaks of the birds jabbing and picking the belly
of the animal, expertly isolating, then tearing the meat from the bone.
They dared me to interrupt their feast, holding their ground, a few
flying away briefly only to make another run. It was a close call—
but then it usually is—as the birds snatched the remains
and stubbornly scuttled to the side of the road.
I had to admire their determination or instinct
or whatever it was that kept them coming back.

Dark Roots

Too often I am reminded and surprised by the light,
surrounded as we are by the enormous black of the universe
where even the stars and planets and galaxies admit
infinitesimal sparkles do little to illuminate the darkness of being,
and living on Earth as long as I have, even briefly,
makes the universe an unfamiliar shape, when I expect
a square, a rectangle, a circle at best, but the will to hold it off
comes wrapping in the dark roots of time,
the dark roots that contain the lights,
when the domain of God is reserved for those
who dare occupy the land with gratitude,
who tenderly pray over its health,
who dance with the ghosts until the dead
populate the plains again despite the white man's slaughter
and the poison rot of chronology and privilege.

CIVIL WAR

A Soldier's Tale

There's a puncture wound in my foot that makes me limp.
Soldiers ask me in which battle I was hit and I lie:
Sometimes it's Chickamauga, and others it's Fort Sanders,
but it was really the sharp stump of a small tree
I stepped on as we were marching to Chattanooga.
The wood pierced my flesh almost to the bone.
Having soles on my boots would have helped.
And I have fought bravely. A shell burst over my head
scattering fragments all around me and into the eyes
of the man standing next to me. Another shell
ripped out the pocket of my jacket, missing my torso entirely.
This last battle was ferocious. We moved through a cornfield,
first left, then right, and after lying on the ground
surrounded by the rotted cobs and empty husks,
we tread at least two miles over hills and valleys,
fording a river knee deep. At the next hill, we took fire,
and a good portion of our battery was extinguished. Again,
the shells landed all around me, only scattering dirt in my face
as I lay on the earth. The rebels came at us with an American flag
yelling, "Don't you shoot on your own," and we stood at attention
until they were right on us. Retreating to the hill under a storm
of shell and shot, we mustered what remained, finding under
the dark shade of a towering oak the lifeless form of a drummer
boy, flaxen hair and blue eyes, a delicate body, the bullet hole
bloodied in the middle of his forehead, a perfect circle.
His eyes were half open and a bright smile filled his face.
This is how to end. This is how to continue, as I dropped
myself onto the ground and went to sleep.

Composition in Black and White

Composition in black and white
LOC original medium: 1 negative: glass: wet collodion.
Dunker Church, a small white cottage set against
the dark woods, and in the foreground a horse
stretched under and supporting the canon that the dead
soldiers must have worked in vain as the dark blue coats
charged into their bodies with bayonets mounted,
the muzzle-loaded rifles hot and clouded with smoke,
and then the screams, and the agony, and the fight to the ground
which took their blood, and their flesh, and their gray

which are spread into a delta aimed toward the disabled artillery,
faces up to the sky, stretched flat against the earth, aimed
toward the church from which maybe a figure emerges
looking at the ground because to see would mean to call
the soldiers dead, would mean to call them something other
than the formation they had been.

Dirt Eater

Every time I see him, my stomach burns,
a weevil chewing into a boll
and so I will have it no more.
House-slave dresses like a white man,
struts and sneers at me like a white man
I ain't taking him no more.

Coming in from the fields at night,
I get down on my knees in the dirt,
scrape the earth with my nails
and take the clay into my mouth.
I chew and chew and cannot break
it down, so I swallow it whole
over and over again until it settles
in my belly to dampen the fire:
white clay, red clay, brown and gray
until sugar and molasses could never
taste as sweet. I have to keep eating,
I have to keep eating until the day I go home

> *Swing low, sweet chariot*
> *Coming for to carry me home*

choking and suffocating on the thick clods.

Master caught me and I went silent,
he covered my face with tin,
one narrow slit in front of my mouth,
a few small holes under my nose
and the necklace of spikes and hooks
securing it all to my head. And the heat
of days laboring under the sun
sears the metal to my skin, rips off
the flesh when the mask is removed
bone bare, still alive.

Witness

I needed to watch him die. I needed to watch his soul.
It was not a big fight, just Fort Sanders, Tennessee.
I had already put three in the ground,
tiny angels only a few months old,
down by the brook and under the willow
I witnessed their bodies surrender to earth
and although they were born with sin,
I saw them carried off by the Lord into the clouds.

Lookaway! Lookaway!

Then Henry at twenty-five grabbed up his rifle
and promised his allegiance to the Rebel cause
even though we did not have any slaves.
Nights, I looked into the fire and
smoke and I know I saw him marching to battle
along with the other brave boys singing

I wish I was in the land of cotton

all the way to the front lines where I know he fought
hard and tangled with the enemy bayonet

In Dixie's Land where I was born

the blade slicing his chest and the blood streaming
from his heart until his gray coat turned red,
his face black with powder, his eyes closing to sleep.

Lookaway! Lookaway!
Lookaway! Dixie Land.

I needed to know, and I imagined he spoke to a portrait
of his wife and son, clutched in his fist as the soldiers hurried
past him, cutting down one another, shot flying, falling
around him, stumbling, screaming—
I ain't afraid to die! I'm goin home.

I wish I was in the land of cotton
Old times there are not forgotten
Lookaway! Lookaway!

But then I did not see him fall, and I did not see a sign.
When I knelt down to pray for him, I only heard my voice

Lookaway! Lookaway!
Lookaway! Dixie Land.

Undertaking

Up on the Potomac, guns popped and cracked at Point of Rocks,
close enough to us crossing at White's Run that we feared
our mission was over before it had started. We did not mind
sacrificing our safety to help our boys because our cause is just,
our cause is this way of life we were promised by our maker
as God made the covenant with Abraham, Isaac, and Jacob,
these hills, these rivers, these crops, this is our Promised Land.

As we returned from collecting boots and clothing for our soldiers,
we found the Union guards had stationed at the river
making it necessary for us to retreat. Under our hoop skirts
the supplies weighed us down, but we reached the Dickerson's
and went about hiding the goods in the walls of the dwelling.
Still, they arrested us, and nights in the Old Capitol Prison
spent in prayer and conspired how to give the Union soldiers fits
when we were sent free. Three weeks we waited and then released
back to our undertaking, and the Lord our Father watched over us
on our little trip back to the Potomac, rushing past a corpse or two,
and at Edward's Ferry, helping us balance and bear heavy loads,
while beneath us the otherwise calm water swirled in its current.

Retreat

They came for me with a bloody hook tailored from a once busy bayonet,
now called into service to tend to the fallen.
The field was glutted with blackened, bloated and festering bodies
of men and boys, their weapons of war, torn coats and bare feet.
I felt my torso jerk when the steel seized my belt,
my back scraping the dirt and dismembered limbs, stray caps
on my way to a shared shallow grave.
I heard hoof beats and boots pounding in my ears,
the sky the color of the ocean rocking
and voices whispering, echoing, fading into the woods.
You see, the soldiers were leaving the field to the dead
and the dying, and not being able to distinguish between the two.

Surrender

I prayed for a rout. Even in battle,
soldiers have eyes, but we were top notch,
dead-eye shots, nimble, smart. In my pocket
a white flag prepared, and until it could wave,
my rifle jammed, I passed out from fatigue,
I became separated from my boys
as we scrambled into position, I carried
a wounded solder back to camp in the pitch
of battle. I slipped to the back of the lines,
I offered myself to the enemy but was refused
by forces greater than either army. Finally

I got myself lost in the woods, fighting
the underbrush, the wind, the rain,
every tree was a soldier with a gun.
My face scratched by briars
trickled with blood, and with each step
I left a trail of desertion with every broken twig.
And then no more popping of guns and cannon.
The birds were silent, the wind and rain
withdrew, and my body was shattered
in the wilderness.

Farewell

What is mine I give to you
in the early days of spring
beneath the budding dogwood,
its white petals bursting through their shells,
I fall and leave my body for the earth,
for the holy flocks
to pick my bones clean.

THIN PLACES

Annunciation

It would have been early spring,
the young girl grinding wheat to flour,
the dishes of beans, nuts, and eggs
spread on the table beside the knife,
and the small dark olives shaken from the trees,
pressed into oil for lamps and meals.
Bits of everyday news at the well,
and the children born
and then tucked into the war-torn land.
This is how the small village girl prepares,
with the balm of small joys and sorrows,
while curled in her under the plain cloth,
spiral galaxies, a faint halo of still forming stars.

Prayer I

I must sing a song of praise for my enemy
who unknowingly drove me into your arms,
and into your light, as the light of the sun

drew me to the water's edge where the spirits'
sighs drifted up from under the surface,
flowered water lilies the velvet vestments of their souls,

and to the blue heron silently waiting in the shallows,
patient, still, to know the sharp and seamless
rapid thrust of the spear-like bill seize prey,

and to stand on the shore admiring its beauty
in the life of its moment before the fish entered,
the passage of one living thing into another.

Prayer II

We assume silence at side of the dying.
What else could the soul possibly want?
How much the tongue demanded.
How much the heart insisted.
The body knows its death. The lungs flooding,
hands searching the flesh for vein and pulse,
hands dreaming of what is past and lost:
It is when the slender shafts of light
finally disturb the air of the sick room;
it is the soul no longer denying the call.
Sent waiting, and falling, and rising,
the last breath.

Prayer IV

What will I do with my flooding dreams
of your golden smile, your smile tangling
me into the summer field of your hair,
those brilliant yellow poppies and soft dark eyes?
First, I placed stones in my shoes
and walked to you across the desert for days.
Next, I fed from a tree of withering figs
until the fruit twisted and rotted into my sides.
Then, I confused them with your silence,
the demon that parches my tongue,
words still forming in the darkness to be eaten.

Answer

I know how things sink in,
permeate the moss and lichen bark
to the oaken core, saturate the cells
of longing that once connected
perish yet leave their walls intact
those hollow, consecrated pathways
filling with water that clings to thin tissues
of the only life it knows.

Earthly Reward

I crawled into the desert
and saw the thick cuticle of my heart,
alone and exposed, clinging to the surface of the sand,
the veins reduced to spines
from which only the deep, red corolla surmounted
by a shaving brush of stamens, flowered,
and flowering.
The sign of temptation
and the sign of resistance
and the sign of life.

Praise the Every Day

It is not necessary for you to always be the light
because it only took the first spark of the candle
to cast you into the shadow of all you have been
and of all that you will be, where you step
from the cave of memory into the forest
to walk through the figures of the leaves
covering the ground and inch by inch
to step into forgetting
the distracted phone call to a friend,
the misplaced words on the page,
the hurried drive through the silver rain,
who and what it was you were supposed to love,
and remember the whole heart you were given,
the passionate kiss always forming,
neither genus nor species nor type,
the symbol of the rose and the rose,
the bud and the bloom.

What Light Can Do

Here is what light can do.
It travels the distance we agree
equals a sum we cannot conceive
without the aid of something far more abstract,
and in it, we see a rainbow or a god
or a sign or a predictor of mood;
we see plants drink in particles of rays
sometimes nurturing sometimes destroying
the delicate organ of the tree, the grasses
the fruits, the ornamentals

and it illuminates a temple of cut block
the gradual brilliance of time
the stone body of a feathered snake
tail to head its linear journey down
the pyramid stairs, jaws open
for the blood and smoke that fill the night.

Caroline Malone was born and lives in the foothills of the Great Smoky Mountains in East Tennessee. A graduate of The University of Tennessee with a B.A. in English and Classics, she earned the MFA in Writing and Literature from the Bennington Writing Seminars. Her poems have appeared in *Boulevard, The Dos Passos Review, Women's Voices, Women Period, Heartwood,* and others. The collection *Dark Roots* explores the meaning of family, heritage, and identity.

Currently, she teaches writing and literature at South College in Knoxville, TN. She also plays Irish traditional music on the bouzouki, mandolin, guitar, concertina, and fiddle.

www.ingramcontent.com/pod-product-compliance
Lightning Source LLC
LaVergne TN
LVHW051610080426
835510LV00020B/3227